THE HISTORY OF
COMMUNICATIONS

MICHAEL JAY

Thomson Learning
New York

CONTENTS

First published in the United States in 1995 by
Thomson Learning,
115 Fifth Avenue, New York, NY 10003

First published in 1994 by Wayland (Publishers) Limited

U.S. version copyright © 1995 Thomson Learning

U.K. version copyright © 1994 Wayland (Publishers) Limited

Library of Congress Cataloging-in-Publication Data
Jay, Michael.
 The history of communications / Michael Jay.
  p.   cm.
 Includes bibliographical references and index.
 ISBN 1-56847-254-4
 1. Communication—History—Juvenile literature.
[1. Communication—History.] I. Title. II. Series: Science
discovery (New York, N.Y.)
P91.2.J37
384'.09—dc20   94-36757

Printed in Italy
384 JAY

Acknowledgments
Concept David Jefferis
Text editor and picture research Michael Brown
Illustrations Peter Bull, Robert Burns, and James Robins
Cover design Norman Berger, U.S.A.

Picture credits
Apple Computers 46; *Boeing Aerospace* 24; *Bridgeman Art Library*
6(T); *British Telecom* 4; *Peter Brown* 6(BL); *Delta Archive* 5, 8, 9(R),
10, 12(T), 13, 14, 15, 18, 19, 22, 23, 27, 28, 29(R), 32, 33, 34, 42, 47;
Hulton-Deutsch Collection 26; *Mat Irvine* 40; *Mary Evans Picture Library*
16; *National Maritime Museum* 12(BL); *Redferns/Suzi Gibbons* 19(T);
Science Photo Library 9(T), 20, 25(TL,TR), 30, 31, 34(TL), 35, 36, 37,
39, 41, 44; *Sharp Electronics* 29(BL); *Sony Corporation* 27;
Southernprint Ltd. 11; *The British Museum* 7; *The Science Museum* 16,
21
Cover: The capture of the Intelsat VI communications satellite by
astronauts Richard J. Hieb, Thomas D. Akers, and Pierre J. Thuot of the
space shuttle *Endeavour.* Courtesy of the National Aeronautics and
Space Administration.

3/01

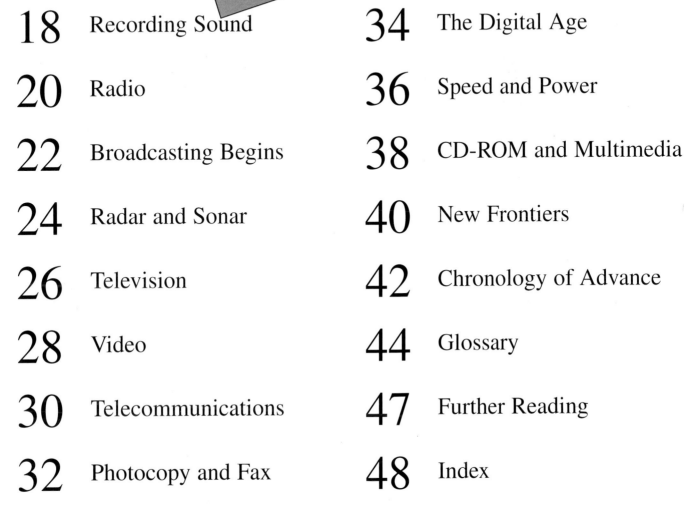

☀ INTRODUCTION

Communications are something we use every day – we speak to people, write down messages, use the telephone, and watch television. But it is easy to take these things for granted, without thinking about how they developed. These developments are what this book is all about.

There have been three major improvements in ways of communicating – the development of the written word, the invention of the printing press, and the invention of electronic machines that have created the telecommunications world of today. Easy communications have created an explosion of knowledge—so much so that we now live in a new age, the Information Age.

We will look at these and other developments and the changes they may bring to our lives in the future.

▶ Stations like this are used to send and receive radio signals to and from communications satellites high in orbit above Earth.

⬤ COMMUNICATING IDEAS

Communications means the exchange of ideas and information among living things. In the animal kingdom a cat fluffs up its fur and hisses to frighten an enemy. A gorilla may beat its breast to declare dominance over a rival. A male moth may find a mate by detecting a chemical released by a female moth many miles away.

We humans first developed languages as a way of expressing ourselves, then we created ways of recording the meanings permanently as the written word. These twin "inventions" have enabled us to communicate complex ideas and information to one another. Just as important, the written word enables us to remember ideas.

Technical advances over the last 400 years or so have produced reliable television and telephone links over long distances, letting people and machines exchange information at the speed of light – 186,282 miles per second – across the world and even out into space. Newspapers, magazines, books, television, movies, and now computer networks allow information to be communicated worldwide in a matter of moments.

▶ A tiny selection of the thousands of newspapers and magazines currently published around the world.

ANCIENT ALPHABETS

Piecing together the story of the written word is a job for archaeologists, researchers of old civilizations. There are huge gaps in our knowledge of how the earliest written languages developed – they were forgotten long before anyone began to take an interest in ancient history. Much of our present knowledge is based on work started by the researchers of the nineteenth century, and some discoveries have been made by sheer chance.

The 20,000-year-old paintings on the walls of a cave at Lascaux in southern France are not writing as such, but they were certainly communications – colorful paintings of hunting scenes that showed stags, horses, bison, and other animals. The cave was discovered by accident in September, 1940, by a group of schoolchildren out on a rabbit hunt with their dog. The dog fell down a hole, and when one of the boys scrambled down to rescue the dog, he found himself surrounded by strange, prehistoric paintings.

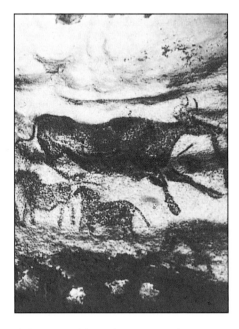

▲ The prehistoric cave painters of Lascaux showed many animals, including these bison.

◀ Ancient Egyptian carvings on temple pillars. The Egyptians were among the first people to develop sophisticated writing.

Finding out what early writings actually mean is a task that is just like cracking a secret code. Sometimes, lettering looks like something that is already understood; other times, inspired guesswork has to be used. The Rosetta Stone is one of the most famous writings. It was discovered by chance by a French soldier in 1799, during the 1798-1801 Napoleonic invasion of Egypt. Chiseled into the slab of stone – named after the place where it was found – were three sets of mysterious scripts, one a type of Greek, the others ancient Egyptian picture lettering, known as hieroglyphics. Experts in France thought the scripts were translations of the same words, but the trouble was, no one understood any of them.

An 18-year-old French scholar named Jean-François Champollion (1790-1832) thought he had a clue, because some of the shapes in the Rosetta Stone's inscriptions looked like Coptic, one of the languages he had already learned as a researcher on ancient Egypt. He had advice and help from many sources, but it was his knowledge of Coptic that enabled him – after fourteen years' effort – to decode the writing on the 2,000-year-old stone and discover the hidden meaning. It was a message from the Egyptian priesthood honoring Ptolemy V, the king who ruled them in 196 B.C. Champollion's work was remarkable because the shapes of the ancient inscriptions were nothing like the alphabetical letters we use today. Ours is the Roman alphabet, itself developed from earlier Greek and Phoenician writings.

 ## THE BRAILLE ALPHABET

The credit for raised writing that blind people could read with their fingers belongs to Frenchman Valentin Haüy (1745-1822). According to one story, Haüy got the idea from seeing how a blind person could tell different piano keys by touch; another story says that a too-heavily printed business card gave him a clue. Either way, Haüy decided on a type style and size, and the first book with raised lettering was printed in 1784. The system that is now used was invented by another Frenchman, Louis Braille (1809-1852), in 1829. Braille used a system of raised dots, similar to the patterns on dominoes. In 1854, Braille was adopted as the official French reading system for the blind. In 1932, Standard English Braille was adopted for worldwide use.

☀ MAKING PAPER

▲ Paper comes in every color, shade, and thickness. Here are just a few kinds of paper you can get in a good stationery store.

Having a written alphabet was a major achievement, but chiseling out shapes into a block of stone or clay is not an easy way of recording a mark. Papyrus was a major improvement: because it was lightweight, it could be stored and transported easily. Papyrus was an Egyptian invention that was first used some 5,000 years ago. Strips of pith were removed from the middle of tall, reedlike papyrus plants that grew along the banks of the Nile River. The Egyptians laid the pith strips side by side, then covered them with a second layer, glued diagonally on top. The resulting sheet was then carefully pressed, dried, and polished, ready for use.

It was the Chinese who came up with the material we still use today – paper. No one knows the exact story, but tradition names Ts'ai Lun, who was a court official to the Chinese emperor, as the person who first made paper, in A.D. 105. Among his ingredients were bits of tree bark, old rags, and fish nets. Ts'ai Lun is thought to have gotten his idea from watching a type of wasp make a thin-shelled nest from tiny flecks of wood fiber, chewing them to make them workable. Ts'ai Lun's paper turned out to be a winner, outperforming silk cloth as a writing surface.

Once papermaking became common in China, the technique spread to other parts of the world. Arabs learned the secret in the eighth century from prisoners they had taken during raiding trips. Papermaking spread slowly into Europe, though for centuries it was made only by hand. The process was much the same as the one the ancient Chinese had used. A wood frame with a wire mesh was dipped into a porridgelike mixture of tiny wood chips and water. The mesh was lifted out, and when the water drained away, a thin layer of wood fibers remained. This was turned out and left to dry; the end result was a sheet of paper. Wood has proved to be the best material for general use, though many other things can be used, including cotton, grass, linen, and even rice.

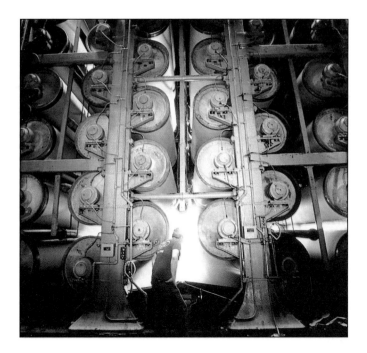

▲ **Rolls of recycled newsprint being dried before reuse. This paper plant processes about 300,000 tons of wastepaper a year, mainly for newspapers and telephone directories.**

The recycled paper industry is an important one. It has been estimated that just one Sunday edition of the *New York Times* creates some 4,000 tons of wastepaper.

The first machine for making paper in a continuous roll was perfected in France by Louis Robert in 1799. Robert invented a machine that used a continuous flow of raw wood pulp, pumped onto a moving wire mesh belt. The pulp was then squeezed and heated between rollers to remove the water and dry the sheet. After this, it could then be rolled up into a big reel. He took the idea to England, where it was improved and patented by Henry and Sealy Fourdrinier. Today's papermaking machines, though more refined, work in a similar way.

By combining dyes and pigments and varying strength and weight, the world's paper manufacturers can offer an almost infinite variety of paper types, from the finest bleached-white notepaper to tough brown wrapping paper.

 ## PENS AND PENCILS

Reed pens were used by the ancient Egyptians, Greeks, and Romans for writing on papyrus and parchment. They also discovered that they could make marks on wax and clay tablets using a pointed rod. This rod, called a stylus, was often made of bronze or bone. The Romans also used pens made of bronze, some with nibs similar to those of today. Quill pens, usually of swan or goose feathers, were used in Europe from about A.D. 600 and were popular up to the nineteenth century, when they began to be replaced by the newly invented fountain pen.

The first fountain pens were made as early as 1809, but these early models had difficulties with a free-flowing ink supply. It was not until 1884 that a successful fountain pen was made, by an American insurance salesman, Lewis Edson Waterman. It had an ink reservoir in the case, which was filled up with a dropper. Later designs had a rubber bag that could be refilled by suction directly from an ink pot. In 1952, there was even the Schnorkel, which came equipped with an extending tube that dipped into the ink!

The pencil dates from 1565, when German scientist Konrad Gesner came up with the idea of putting a graphite rod in a wooden tube. The pencil was the first real alternative to the quill pen.

A ballpoint pen was first thought up by American John J. Loud in 1888, but it was crude and competed against the fountain pen, which was then new and highly successful. The ballpoint we know today was a 1938 invention from two Hungarians, Ladislao and Georg Biro, who aimed to make a pen that would work cleanly at high altitudes, for use in the British Royal Air Force's new planes. Success lay in the Biros' secret-formula thick ink, which dried almost instantly on contact with paper.

THE PRINTING PRESS

▲ **An early printing press. Moving the big lever controlled the amount of pressure on the paper. Adjusting it correctly to achieve the best finished result was part of a printer's craft.**

 ## A BIG BUSINESS

Printing is a huge industry today, with speedy production being a major requirement. Early mechanical presses printed about 1,100 sheets an hour. The rotary press, patented by Richard Hoe in 1846, speeded things up to 8,000 sheets. By 1865 papers were being printed using continuous reels of paper, which was cut after printing. Using this system, 20,000 sheets per hour (or 12,000 complete newspapers per hour) was possible.

A key development in the history of communications was that of the printing press. Until then, making copies of anything was very slow, done one at a time, by hand.

The Chinese developed the first printing methods in about the sixth century A.D., but it was not for another five hundred years that the idea of movable type was put into practice, again by the Chinese. With movable type, individual characters were carved into hard wood. The pieces could be arranged as required, then rearranged afterward for use time and time again.

But the credit for the start of printing in Europe goes to the fifteenth-century German, Johannes Gutenberg. He reinvented the Chinese idea of movable type and in 1456 printed two huge volumes of the Bible for the city of Mainz, Germany. He used cast metal for the movable letters, which was a huge improvement over wood, allowing sharp reproduction and much longer life before wearing out.

The print revolution, and the knowledge explosion it fueled, spread rapidly across Europe. By 1476, wool merchant William Caxton had set up the first printing press in Great Britain, bringing the machine across the North Sea from Bruges, Belgium, where he had lived for several years. For the first time ever, using Gutenberg's invention, books, leaflets, and soon the first newspapers could be produced quickly, cheaply, and in large numbers, allowing knowledge to be spread widely.

▲ A modern full-color printing press, capable of printing thousands of large sheets an hour. They are bound into book form by a binder. Machine-printing was not invented until the early nineteenth century, and the first newspaper to be printed this way was *The Times* of London in 1814. Newspaper printing remained almost entirely black-and-white, right up until the 1980s. Even today, newspapers generally use color sparingly.

▼ A color printing press builds up a picture one stage at a time by using four colored inks: cyan (blue), magenta (red), yellow, and black. Overlaying these, one after another, creates a color image. The full-color effect is achieved by printing thousands of tiny dots. If you look at a printed picture – such as one on a page of this book – through a magnifying glass, you can see how the dots are arranged.

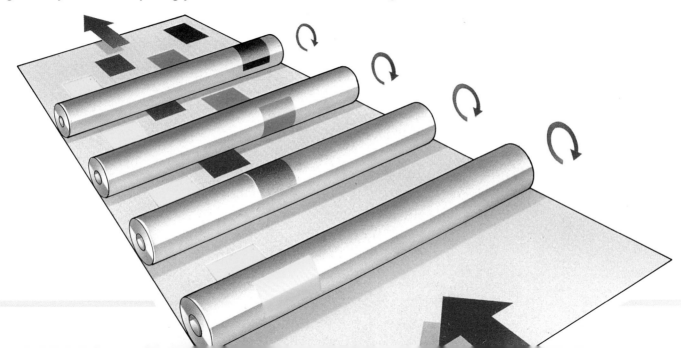

SENDING MESSAGES

Although the printing press spread knowledge widely and fairly quickly, it became important to improve the speed of sending information. Before today's electronic links, the need for speed inspired many inventions and developments.

For short distances, signal flags were a good option and were particularly useful at sea. During naval battles, secret codes were necessary for sending messages and battle orders to keep the enemy from knowing what was going on. Otherwise, simple semaphore—the changing positions of a pair of flags representing letters of the alphabet—could be used.

Over longer distances many systems have been used, from the smoke signals of American Indians to message-carrying homing pigeons. Horseback relay systems were used by the Mongols of Asia and later by the Pony Express riders of nineteenth-century America. But the first real technological breakthrough was by an enterprising French engineer, Claude Chappe.

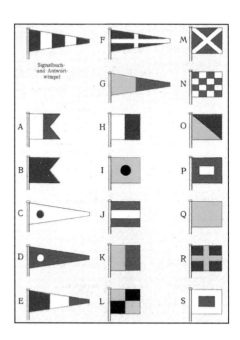

▲ This page from an old German naval manual shows a range of signal flags, each representing a letter of the alphabet.

◄ Naval signal flags were used in battles between France and Great Britain in the Napoleonic Wars. Here, coded orders and messages fly from the rigging.

Chappe used the optical power of the telescope as an essential part of his plan for a communications system for the French army in the 1790s. His team built a large number of towers, each one just in sight of the other. Depending on the landscape, this could be up to about 12 miles or so. Movable wooden arms were mounted on top of each tower, the arms changing position in a code system that represented letters of the alphabet. The message was passed on, relay-style, by a lookout in the next tower peering through his telescope, reading the positions of the arms. This second tower's arms were adjusted accordingly and read in turn by the lookout in the third tower in the chain, and so on.

Chappe's optical semaphore had many drawbacks – it was expensive to run, since all the towers had to be permanently manned, and bad weather was a problem. But when skies were clear, messages could be sent and received faster than ever before – the record time for one short message on Chappe's system was just three minutes over a distance of some 500 miles.

▲ One of Claude Chappe's semaphore towers. The first message was sent a distance of some 150 miles, between Lille and Paris, on August 15, 1794. By the time Chappe died in 1805, his system covered much of France, with a 3,100-mile network of 556 stations. It was in regular use for another 50 years.

THE ELECTRIC TELEGRAPH

Useful as Chappe's system was, there was strong competition from people with machines that used electricity, then still a new and rather mysterious force. Researchers found that electricity traveled very quickly along metal wires, so the idea of using it for sending messages was a good one. Not all suggestions were very practical however—Francisco Salva from Spain thought up a plan that involved operators sending and receiving coded electric shocks! A better solution was one devised by Georges Lesage, who in 1774 built a machine that flashed messages between rooms in his residence in Geneva, Switzerland. It was too complex though, as each letter of the alphabet had to have its own separate wire.

Various projects were devised in the early years of the nineteenth century, and the inventor of the first practical electric telegraph was Baron Paul Schilling of Germany. His equipment impressed the Russian czar Nicholas I enough that a Schilling telegraph was built in 1832 to connect the government offices in St. Petersburg with the imperial palace some distance away in Peterhof.

▲ Samuel Morse devised a dot-dash code system with his assistant, Alfred Vail. Morse also perfected an electrical relay for the telegraph itself, an idea based on earlier talks with a fellow American, Joseph Henry. The relay behaved as a signal booster, enabling signals to travel long distances without needing massive power plants.

▼ Lesage's equipment could send messages short distances. Its complexity made it impractical.

Meanwhile in Great Britain, physicists William Cooke and Charles Wheatstone also worked on the electric telegraph. In 1837 they demonstrated their equipment to the directors of a railroad company. At that time the railroads were the fastest means of travel, and the speedy telegraph was presented as a good way to improve safety by showing if there were holdups or accidents farther along the line. In 1839, a 13-mile telegraph line was activated, with much success.

The early telegraphs were usually laid next to railroads and roads. At first, they stopped at borders between countries, where messages were jotted down then sent on again. This caused so many delays that, in 1852, it was agreed that international lines could be built. Apart from railroad companies sending safety instructions and individuals sending messages, the booming newspaper industry became a major user of the telegraph. Headline stories that once might have taken days or weeks to arrive from distant countries now arrived in hours or minutes. Baron Paul Julius von Reuter was among the first to use the telegraphs for news gathering, and the agency he created in 1851 is still in the news business.

▲ **By the mid-nineteenth century, telegraphy was a booming business. Here, dozens of operators work in the central Paris telegraph office.**

In North America, telegraph lines marched side by side with the railroads, from east to west, across the continent, driving the short-lived Pony Express company out of business in 1862. In 1860, this horseback relay service had been the quickest way of sending messages the 2,000-mile distance between St. Joseph, Missouri, which was the end of the railroad, and San Francisco. Samuel Morse's code system became the standard way of sending messages on the American telegraphs. It was a brilliantly simple idea that used combinations of dots and dashes to represent letters and numbers. It was fairly easy to learn and quick to use, and eventually Morse code became the world standard.

▶ **Cooke and Wheatstone's telegraphs used magnetic needles that swung into various positions as current passed down the telegraph wire. The wire ran beside the railroad; the telegraph machines were in the stations.**

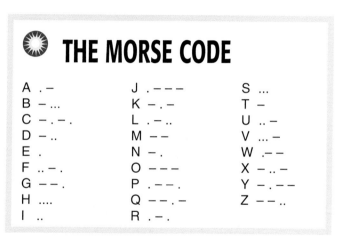

✺ THE MORSE CODE

A	. –	J	. – – –	S	. . .
B	– . . .	K	– . –	T	–
C	– . – .	L	. – . .	U	. . –
D	– . .	M	– –	V	. . . –
E	.	N	– .	W	. – –
F	. . – .	O	– – –	X	– . . –
G	– – .	P	. – – .	Y	– . – –
H	. . . .	Q	– – . –	Z	– – . .
I	. .	R	. – .		

THE TELEPHONE

The idea of sending the voice over a distance dates back to 1667, when Englishman Robert Hooke suggested joining two cans with a long piece of taut string. It made a good toy, but was no good over long distances.

The invention of the telephone came shortly after the telegraph system was well established. Researchers then tackled the problems of sending the complex patterns of the human voice down a wire, instead of staying with systems such as the Morse code. The man who succeeded, though by only a few hours, was Scottish-born Alexander Graham Bell (1847-1922). At the same time another inventor, Elisha Gray, was racing toward publishing his ideas; but Bell gets the credit because he got to the American patent office a short time before Gray!

▲ Alexander Graham Bell was born in Scotland, emigrating to the United States in 1871. Apart from his pioneering scientific work, he gave music lessons and taught deaf people how to speak.

▶ A replica of Bell's first telephone transmitter. Bell was helped with advice from Joseph Henry and assisted by Thomas Watson. Bell and Watson were testing a new telegraph transmitter designed to send several messages at the same time – the first words were sent accidentally when Watson heard Bell shout that he had spilled acid down his clothes!

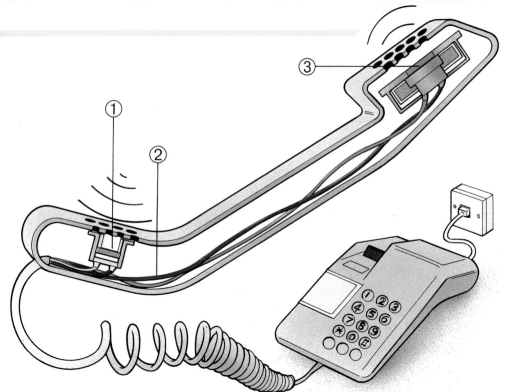

◀ **Many telephones use a carbon microphone. As you speak, sound waves from your mouth move a very thin, metal diaphragm in the mouthpiece (1), which in turn presses against carbon granules. The varying movements, though very small, are enough to create a changing electric current, which is passed down the telephone line (2). Varying electric signals received by an earpiece (3) move an electromagnet, which vibrates another diaphragm. The result is the sound of your voice in the other person's ear.**

Bell's first telephone was based on the electromagnet, two of which were joined by wires. To use the machine, you spoke into a funnel-shaped chamber, in which the vibrations from your voice shook a thin, flat sheet of metal called a diaphragm. These small movements caused changes in the magnetic field of an electromagnet. The varying forces were then sent as an electrical signal to the receiver. This early system was soon replaced by the carbon microphone (shown in the diagram) which was much more efficient and was largely responsible for the telephone's success.

Bell worked hard at letting people know about the telephone, both in America where he had perfected it and in Europe. American response was dramatic, but the Europeans were not quite as enthusiastic. The existing telegraph system was regarded by many as being quite sufficient, especially since the sound quality of the early telephones was not good. Telephones were expensive to introduce: each one needed its own connection, the wires had to be of better quality than telegraph lines, and telephone poles were prone to storm damage.

Even so, it was only a matter of time before the telephone caught on. In 1880 there were barely 33,000 telephones in the world, but ten years later there were more than 400,000. Today, there are so many that the exact figure is not known, but it is probably around the one billion mark.

✹ TELEPHONE EXCHANGES

The first telephones were connected to one another in pairs, with no way of linking to others. The first telephone exchanges were built to expand the system. Local lines went into an exchange office, where operators rerouted calls by switching sockets on a big board. To make a long-distance call, you always had to go through the operator.

As telephones grew in number, it became necessary to have lists of subscribers, and the first telephone directory was printed in New Haven, Connecticut, in 1878. Today, the most advanced directories, such as the French Minitel system, are entirely computer-based.

RECORDING SOUND

The world's first recorded words were "Mary had a little lamb," spoken by American inventor Thomas Alva Edison (1847-1931). With this poetic line, Edison made listening to recorded sound as easy as printing had made reading a book. Edison's list of inventions is still a record-breaker for one man—he took out no fewer than 1,097 patents. Most of them were improvements of existing machines, but sound recording was his own, unique contribution to improving the world's communications.

Edison called his machine the phonograph. It was an early version of the record player. Instead of flat disks, the phonograph used small cylinders, covered in a thin coat of wax. A sensitive needle recorded sound vibrations as a wriggling groove in the rotating cylinder. To play the recording, the needle tracked the same groove, replaying the sounds through a pair of headphones, or, later, through a trumpet-shaped horn. No electricity was needed for the first phonographs because the cylinder turned by clockwork.

▲ Thomas Edison started off his inventing career early—by the age of ten, he had a fully equipped basement chemistry laboratory. His inventions included telegraphic printers, the phonograph, and improvements to the telephone. Edison's phonograph used wax cylinders for recording and playing.

1

2

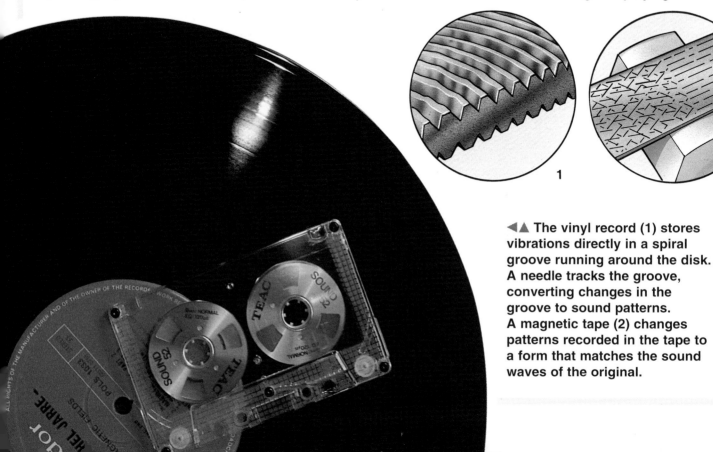

◀◀ The vinyl record (1) stores vibrations directly in a spiral groove running around the disk. A needle tracks the groove, converting changes in the groove to sound patterns. A magnetic tape (2) changes patterns recorded in the tape to a form that matches the sound waves of the original.

After Edison's phonograph, sound recording, using disks and tapes, become a big industry. The magnetic tape recorder was invented in 1898 by Valdemar Poulsen from Denmark, who demonstrated his "telegraphone" at the 1900 Paris Exhibition, a huge show held to celebrate the dawn of the twentieth century. The machine recorded sounds as magnetized patterns on a moving steel tape. The telegraphone was the forerunner of today's familiar tape recorder, but the idea had to wait for the electronic amplifier to be developed before it became practical. Poulsen's machine was also the very first telephone answering machine—it was originally devised as a message-taker for the telephone, a device that was then less than 25 years old. As well as using tape, Poulsen was also the first to use a thin coating of powder that could be magnetized.

The tape recorder took a long time to become really popular, however—it was not until the 1950s, when cheap and tough plastic-based tapes became widely available, that home tape recording took off. With the 1960s-era compact cassette, prerecorded music tapes sealed the beginning of the end for the vinyl record.

▲ In a modern recording studio, sound engineers have total control over the finished product. Sounds from voices and instruments can be adjusted, mixed, and remixed, until exactly the right effect is achieved.

▲ Before power amplifiers were invented, record players used horn loudspeakers. The horn increased sound picked up by the needle as a megaphone amplified a voice.

⊛ RADIO

In 1887, German physicist Heinrich Rudolf Hertz showed that radio waves—invisible waves similar to light waves—exist. His experimental equipment proved that a spark of electricity also sends out a radio wave, like the ripples in a pond when a stone is thrown in it. What's more, he discovered that the waves can be bent and reflected like light, even though they can't be seen. And, most importantly, radio waves are fast—they travel at the speed of light.

But though Hertz and other scientists performed many experiments, there seemed to be no practical use for radio waves. It was engineer Guglielmo Marconi (1874-1937), from Bologna, Italy, whose discoveries led to the radios we use today. He started experimenting in his Bologna house in 1894 and soon succeeded in sending and receiving radio-wave transmissions over a distance of about one and a half miles. He tried to get the Italian government interested but was turned down. In 1896 he went to Great Britain where the potential of the equipment impressed Sir William Preece, the post office chief engineer.

⊛ BEATING THE STORMS

When Marconi and his team were preparing equipment for the first transatlantic radio message, they ran into trouble with bad weather. Storms broke the fragile antennas, and in Newfoundland high-flying kites were used instead. To travel such a distance, the signals bounced off layers in the upper atmosphere.

▼ **Marconi, photographed with his equipment**

The British government was slow in making up its mind about providing backing however, and Marconi went on to form his own company, the Wireless Telegraph and Signal Company in 1897. Progress was rapid as Marconi improved his equipment, and in 1901 he managed to send a signal from Cornwall in England to Newfoundland, Canada, a distance of 2,140 miles. Marconi called his device the wireless telegraph, because no wires were used between the sender and receiver. Morse code was used to send messages.

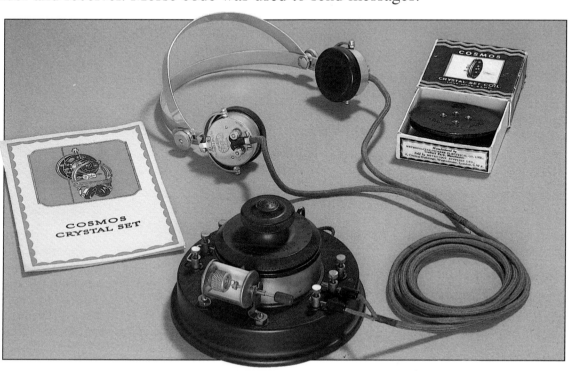

► Messages were heard on early radio receivers using a pair of headphones. Electronic amplifiers, with their ability to power large loudspeakers, were not generally available until the 1930s.

A sensational murder case sealed the success of radio communication. In 1910, the ocean liner *Montrose* sailed across the Atlantic with murderer Dr. Hawley Crippen as one of the passengers. He was fleeing from justice in Great Britain to a new life in Canada. Unknown to Crippen, the British police contacted the ship's captain by wireless, then boarded a faster ship to overtake the *Montrose*. Crippen's day-to-day shipboard life was splashed in newspapers on both sides of the Atlantic, without his knowing a thing about it. And no one was more surprised than Crippen when police eventually boarded the *Montrose* to arrest him!

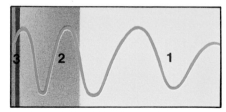

▲ Radio waves (1) are part of the electromagnetic spectrum, which also includes infrared (2), which we feel as heat, and visible light (3).

Two years later, another liner, the *Titanic*, sank on its maiden voyage after hitting an iceberg in the middle of the Atlantic. Hundreds of lives were lost, partly because the radio operator aboard the nearest ship was off duty and did not hear the distress signals from the doomed ship. After the disaster, all ships were required to have a wireless and an operator on duty constantly, in case of emergency calls.

BROADCASTING BEGINS

In 1906 many wireless operators were surprised to hear music instead of Morse code coming out of their headphones. This radio broadcast, by American physicist Reginald Fessenden, was the first thing anyone heard at long range besides crackles and Morse code. Fessenden's equipment had a range of about two hundred miles, but, despite this, it was years before public broadcasting started. Receiving equipment was not yet reliable enough for mass production, and no one had thought of using the radio for interest and entertainment.

But the radio industry was booming as a commercial and emergency system. There were also many amateur radio enthusiasts (known as radio "hams"), and when some European hams started broadcasting entertainment instead of the usual serious fare, people (especially the makers of radio equipment) realized that there might be a big future in such transmissions.

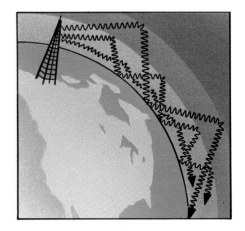

▲ **Long-distance broadcasting was made possible because some types of radio waves bounce off layers in the upper atmosphere. Reception could be a hit-and-miss affair though, because such communications are easily affected by bad weather.**

▶ **Radio was a boom industry from the 1920s on. This 1949 "radiogram" (taken from an advertisement in a magazine of the time) was a popular gadget that combined radio receiver and record player. The nearest thing today is a boom box, which typically has radio, tape, and compact disc functions.**

◀ Inside a transistor radio. An antenna picks up the signal. The electronic components are assembled on a circuit board. The loudspeaker is attached to the plastic case.

The very first public radio station, KDKA of Pittsburgh, Pennsylvania, began transmissions in 1920. In 1928, the British Broadcasting Corporation (BBC) was sending out a mixture of news, theater, and music. European stations filled the airwaves, too. By 1930, radio broadcasting was big business. Today there are thousands of stations, covering everything from rock and classical music to sports and current events.

Radio receivers have come a long way since the primitive equipment available in the 1920s. The invention of the transistor in 1947 by a three-man American team allowed the production of radios that were small and reliable. Before the transistor, radios were mostly big and bulky devices that used fragile and unreliable valves in their circuits. Transistors marked the dawn of the electronic age, as they were cheap to make, tough, and reliable. They are used as switches or to amplify an electric current or voltage.

✺ TRANSISTOR PIONEERS

The transistor, with its triple advantages of small size, low cost, and reliability, fueled the development of the electronic devices we use today. The transistor was developed by William Shockley (1910-1989), with John Bardeen and Walter H. Brattain. These scientists shared the 1956 Nobel Prize in Physics for their pioneering work in the field.

RADAR AND SONAR

The idea for radar dates back to 1904, when German physicist Christian Huelsmeyer suggested using reflected radio waves as an early warning system to prevent ships from colliding at sea. Interesting as the idea was, there were no developments until the 1930s, when it was revived as a form of early warning system to detect enemy planes before they got within bombing range. In World War II, radar became a vital weapon in the armories of the fighting powers.

Radar, which stands for **ra**dio **d**etection **a**nd **r**anging, was first developed by a British team led by Scottish physicist Robert Watson-Watt (1892-1973). By 1936, a chain of radar stations was being built along the south coast of Great Britain. The advantage of the system was that defending fighter planes could stay on the ground until needed and then be directed to the enemy, without wasting time in a midair search.

▲ Ground-based radar is used to monitor aircraft near airports. The radar sends out a powerful pulse of radio energy (shown red in the diagram). Some of this energy is reflected (shown blue) by the aircraft and received by the radar dish. The result is displayed as a glowing "blip" on a radar screen.

▲ The AWACS (Airborne Warning And Command System) jets are among the most important of today's military aircraft. From a cruise height of 32,000 feet, an AWACS can pinpoint hundreds of enemy air and land positions.

The first radar equipment was big and bulky, but before long, radar sets were made small enough to be carried aboard aircraft. Here they were used to detect enemy ships, submarines, and other aircraft, especially at night. Today, virtually all aircraft bigger than light planes carry radar as standard. Weather radar allows the crew of an airliner to steer clear of particularly bad weather. Ground-based radar is used by air traffic controllers to steer planes safely to and from airports. Ships, too, carry radar to steer clear of rocks and other obstructions.

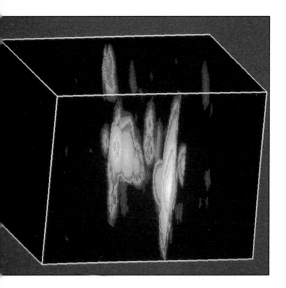

▲ Sonar is an essential piece of equipment for many vessels, from fishing boats to nuclear submarines. This picture shows a computer-generated three-dimensional sonar display, which includes (believe it or not) an image of a fish on the left.

▲ The orange box is a towed sonar. It is about to be released from a research ship. It has a range of about 1.5 miles under water and can penetrate 230 feet through ocean-bottom sediment.

Sonar (from the words **so**und **n**avigation **a**nd **r**anging) is also a system that works by detecting reflections from objects. In this case, the reflections are echoes from short bursts of high-pitched sound, sent out by a transmitter. It was the sinking of the *Titanic* in 1912 that inspired scientists to find a way of detecting icebergs before they could do any damage. Submarine warfare during World War I made this underwater warning system even more vital. French scientist Paul Langevin began experiments in Paris in 1915, and by 1916 he had succeeded in producing ultrasonic (higher than human ears can detect) sound waves that could penetrate up to about two miles under water. With careful tuning, Langevin found that his sonar equipment could detect schools of fish and other underwater objects. It could also be used to measure the depth of the sea under a ship, reducing the risk of running aground in shallow waters.

Sonar systems of today display returning echoes on a video screen. There can be quite an art to understanding the meaning of the ghostly blue-gray image, however—even a trained operator sometimes cannot tell the difference between a submarine and a large whale. Sonar is slower than radar—in water, sound waves travel at little more than 3,200 mph. But despite this, sonar is of more use than even the most powerful radar, because few radio waves travel far under water.

TELEVISION

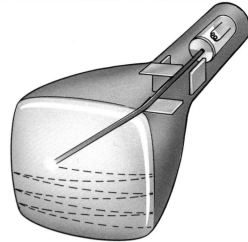

With the success of radio, a major communications target for researchers—transmitting moving pictures as well as sound—developed. There was a precedent for the idea itself: sending "wire" pictures by telegraph had become common. Here, a picture was broken down into thousands of dots, which were transmitted one after another. It was a slow process, however, and could not be used for motion pictures.

In 1926, Scottish electronics pioneer John Logie Baird (1888-1946) came up with the first working television system. It used a spinning disk, combined with a photoelectric cell that changed the varying brightness of the image into electrical signals. The result was a fuzzy picture, that, though much improved over the next few years, lost out to an electronic rival, the iconoscope.

▲ The picture on a conventional TV screen is created by a glowing "flying spot" that moves from side to side. As the spot zigzags down, it creates an image. The process is repeated 25 times a second, so fast that the picture seems to be steady. The spot appears when invisible particles called electrons hit the back of the screen. The screen is coated with a substance that glows briefly when struck by electrons.

▲ John Logie Baird with his experimental mechanical scanning television apparatus

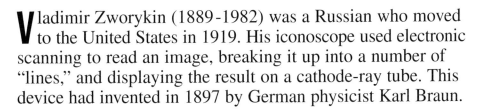

 **The first transistor portable TV set (above) weighed less than 14 pounds. Densely packed electronic components fill the insides of the 1970s portable shown at left, but this type of TV will be a museum piece before long. By the year 2000, almost all conventional cathode-ray picture tubes will have been replaced by flat screens, similar to those on laptop computers.**

Vladimir Zworykin (1889-1982) was a Russian who moved to the United States in 1919. His iconoscope used electronic scanning to read an image, breaking it up into a number of "lines," and displaying the result on a cathode-ray tube. This device had invented in 1897 by German physicist Karl Braun.

Scheduled television service began on May 11, 1928, from station WGY in Schenectady, New York, but at first the programs were only broadcasts of moving images, without entertainment or news value. Broadcast television was almost entirely in black and white until 1953, when the American National Television Systems Committee (NTSC) adopted a color system that split the picture into its primary colors of red, green, and blue, using special mirrors. Electronic picture tubes put out three electric signals that varied with the brightness of these primary colors, and the three signals were combined to form a full-color image by the receiving set.

Today, several broadcasting systems compete with NTSC, including France's SECAM and Germany's PAL. The quality of the pictures is similar (though PAL is generally considered the best), but if you have, say, a PAL TV set, then you cannot pick up NTSC broadcasts. Only special multi-standard receiving equipment pick up all of them.

✺ TELEVISION WORLD

Television has allowed people to share some things in common. Commercially, TV advertising has enabled some manufacturers to make "world brands" of their products. Satellite TV has made it easy to keep up to date with world news, provided that you have a satellite dish (see page 30). In China, however, the rulers have banned such dishes to much of the population, because they fear the unsettling effects of foreign TV programs.

VIDEO

Video is now the most popular way of recording sounds and pictures, especially programs directly from television broadcasts and movies for home replay. The first video recorder was developed in 1956 by a team working for the American Ampex corporation, a company that already made tape-recording equipment.

The video cassette recorder (VCR) stores images as well as sound on magnetic tape. It receives signals from an antenna and records pictures, 25 per second, as diagonal stripes across the tape. The sound is usually recorded at the edge of the tape, separate from the video signal. The first Ampex system used a bulky 50 mm-wide tape, but today home video cassette recorders mostly use the 12.65 mm-wide Home Video System (VHS) tape developed by the J. Victor Company of Japan in the 1970s. There were several competitors for a universal home video system, including rivals from Philips in Holland and Sony in Japan, but the VHS system won the battle, largely because many other electronics manufacturers were allowed to build VHS equipment under license. VHS simply swamped the competition.

▲ Different types of video tape include high-quality professional types (bottom) and home-use VHS and 8 mm (top).

► There are hundreds of different types of video recorders, but they all share similar parts. These include:

1. Video tape
2. Audio recording head
3. Video recording head
4. Guide rollers
5. Erasing head

Owning a VCR was fine, but what if you wanted to record your family and friends? The answer to that, up until the late 1970s, was a home-movie camera, which used narrow, "bootlace" photographic film. Each reel was expensive, lasted just a few minutes, and had to be developed by a special photography lab. Also, the image was often fuzzy and wobbly, and film could break in the projector.

The answer to all this came in the form of domestic video cameras—miniaturized VCRs that included lens and light-sensing electronics in a hand-held package. These came mostly from the big Japanese electronics companies, led by the Sony corporation in 1979. Various video camera ("camcorder") makers tried to outdo one another, but by the 1990s, just two recording formats ruled the camcorder market—VHS and the 8 mm system, from a team of companies headed by Sony. Both systems offer long recording times and the ability to erase and rerecord unwanted material.

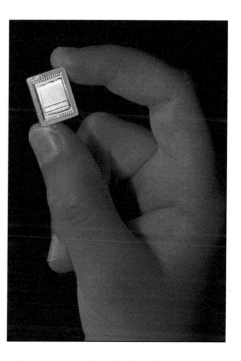

▶ The secret of a camcorder's ability to record light lies behind the lens. This is a tiny CCD chip.

▲ A flat-screen TV monitor replaces the traditional viewfinder on this model, a Sharp ViewCam.

The camcorder's main technical advance is that it uses electronics to record the image. The CCD, or charge coupled device, uses an array of tiny light sensors, anything up to 800,000 on a chip just 17 mm across. As light from the lens falls on each sensor, a small electric current is set up. The change in current gets translated into an electronic signal by complex circuits on the camcorder. The result is recorded onto tape, one frame at a time, in diagonal stripes for later replay. This can be either in the camcorder or through a home VCR.

TELECOMMUNICATIONS

Planet Earth is surrounded by an invisible spider's web of long-distance electronic links that allow you to see TV shows from far-off countries or talk to someone half a world away with no more effort than it takes to speak to someone in the next room.

The story of long-distance communications began in the nineteenth century with the first telegraph systems. Intercontinental links started with the laying of the first transatlantic telegraph cable in 1858. People found the new links essential: by 1885 many more underwater cables had been laid and nearly two million telegrams were sent every week. Amazingly, the first telephone cable across the Atlantic was not laid until 1956; it provided just 36 interference-free telephone lines. A year later the space age began with the launch of the Russian *Sputnik I* space satellite. With this, an idea first suggested in 1945 by science-fiction writer Arthur C. Clarke began to take shape—that of using satellites high above Earth as relay stations for radio messages.

▲ A microwave tower, often used for distances that do not require a satellite.

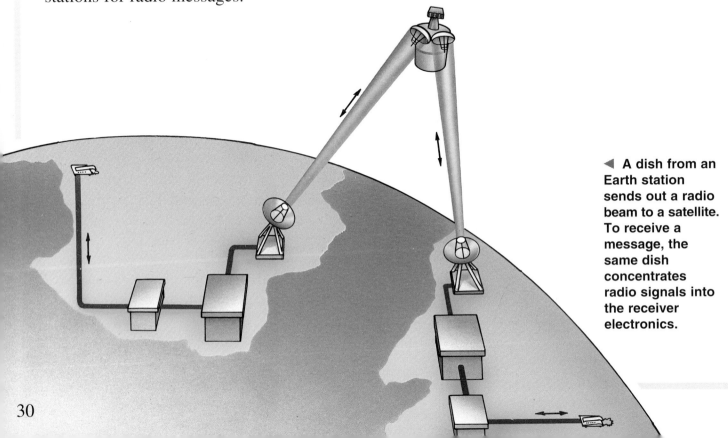

◀ A dish from an Earth station sends out a radio beam to a satellite. To receive a message, the same dish concentrates radio signals into the receiver electronics.

The new age of global communications dawned in 1962 with the launch of the first TV Comsat, or communications satellite, the American *Telstar 1*. This ball-shaped Comsat could relay signals aimed at it from a ground-based transmitter, around the curve of the world to an Earth station waiting to receive the message. *Telstar* first relayed live TV signals across the Atlantic in 1962.

Telstar was followed a year later by *Syncom 1*, which did a similar job but from a higher orbit. This was at a height of some 22,000 miles, an altitude at which a satellite appears to stay in the same spot above the equator. Using just three Comsats in this geostationary orbit – their positions form a huge triangle in space – a message can be sent anywhere on Earth in less than half a second. In fact, if you talk to someone on the other side of the world, the only clue to the distance involved is the very slight delay as you talk to each other. There are now dozens of Comsats in geostationary orbit. They carry thousands of TV and telephone signals every moment of the day.

Back on Earth, microwave links can be used to relay signals over fairly short distances. Microwaves are radio waves that can be very tightly beamed. They travel between towers that are in sight of each other, not unlike an electronic version of Chappe's optical telegraph.

◀ **Comsats have ranged in size from the 3-foot-wide *Telstar* to the Intelsat series, each of which is the size of a truck. Here a Comsat is launched from the cargo bay of the space shuttle *Discovery*. A long-distance telephone call goes from home to an exchange, then to an Earth station, which beams the message into space. The satellite relays the signal across the world.**

PHOTOCOPY AND FAX

Making or sending a copy of a document used to be a fairly complicated affair. If you typed a story, you could use a sheet of coated carbon paper, sandwiched between your "top copy" and the copy sheet. It was a dirty business, and carbon paper was slippery stuff that often dropped between the sheets of paper. Sending a copy over a distance was even less convenient. You could send it by mail and be prepared to wait, or you could send a telegram. This involved either a trip to the telegraph office or arranging for collection by a messenger. The twin inventions of the photocopier and facsimile, or fax, machine changed all that.

Most photocopiers use a process invented in the 1930s by American Chester F. Carlson, who needed a copier that could reproduce not just words, but pictures, too. Carlson was a lawyer who dealt with patent application forms, almost all of which included complex descriptions and diagrams of new gadgets and inventions. Carlson named his process xerography, after the Greek words *xeros*, meaning "dry," and *graphos*, meaning "writing."

▶ The latest copiers can work in color and can also produce special effects, including image distortion.

Carlson's dry copier works by the principle of electrostatic attraction. This is similar to the attraction between a balloon and pieces of paper after the balloon has been rubbed on hair or fabric. Inside the copier a metal plate is given a static charge. The metal conducts electricity only when light shines on it. An image of the document to be copied is focused on the plate, until the plate carries an "electric copy." Black powder called toner is then sprayed at the plate. It sticks to the charged parts and falls off the rest. The toner is then transferred to a sheet of paper pressed against it. A heater finishes off the job by baking the toner.

◄ This blowup shows how a fax machine breaks down a photograph into tiny dots. The fax is widely used—some estimates reckon that nearly three-quarters of telephone calls between countries in the Pacific Ocean area are fax messages, not voice conversations. There are currently about three million fax machines worldwide.

The electronic fax (short for facsimile, or copy) machine uses telephone wires to send messages to other fax machines anywhere in the world. A bright light scans the image, whether words, pictures, or both, but rather than create an exact copy, the fax breaks down the image into rows and rows of tiny dots. These are sent as fax code—like a faster, electronic version of Morse code—down the telephone line to a fax machine at the receiving end. Here, the fax code is received and printed out in lines of dots. Most people, especially those in business, regard the fax as a great help, mainly in sending letters quickly.

The fax first became popular in Japan. As little as ten years ago, most Japanese business was conducted face to face, not on the telephone, with documents written by hand rather than typed. Japanese alphabets contain thousands of picture symbols, and a 1970s typewriter looked more like a full-scale typesetting machine than a desktop device. Communication devices such as the telex, which require typing, were complicated. But the fax enables handwritten letters to be sent with the speed of a phone call.

THE DIGITAL AGE

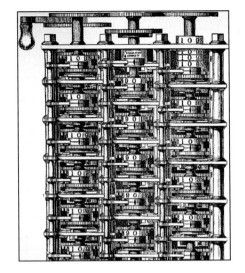

▲ A drawing of a Babbage calculating machine. The machine was never completed: Babbage ran out of money to continue work on the project.

The computer is developing into probably the ultimate communications tool. A laptop word-processing computer was used to write this book, and a desktop computer was used to design its pages. Still other computers were used at various print and production stages. We use computers in every part of our lives, yet all this has come about in little more than the last forty years. How did it all happen?

The idea for computing came about when people realized how much time was involved in adding up long lists of figures. For over 300 years, various inventors tried to make the job quicker and less prone to error by mechanizing it. The first known attempt at building a "mathematics engine" was in 1642, when French mathematician and physicist Blaise Pascal (1623-62) built a mechanical calculating machine. In 1834, Charles Babbage (1792-1871) designed the first machine we might recognize as a computer.

◄ The most powerful early computers were huge. Today, an average laptop computer packs more punch than this room-sized machine of the 1950s.

Babbage was Professor of Mathematics at Cambridge University, England, and was so excited about his invention that he resigned his post to work on the Difference Engine full-time. In 1834, there was no such thing as an electronics industry, so Babbage's machine depended on sets of finely made brass gears to produce answers to problems. Babbage thought up a second machine, the Analytical Engine, which was intended to solve algebra problems as well as simple sums. He worked on this for more than a decade, but he never finished it.

There are various competitors for the title of first modern computer. The first that used a stored program for operation was the Z3 of German Konrad Zuse, in 1941. The machine was used for military aircraft design. Two years later, the first electronic computer, called Colossus, was in use by the British to help crack enemy secret codes. Colossus needed a team of engineers to keep things in working order, one of the jobs being to replace valves, which burned out from time to time. Colossus had 1,500 valves that acted as switches and amplifiers in the circuits of the machine. In 1946, an American team built the 18,000-valve ENIAC, the first digital computer. This used binary code, the counting method that became the standard system.

COMPUTING PIONEER

Charles Babbage was born ahead of his time—the technology that was available in the nineteenth century was not advanced enough for the demands of computer processing. But the idea behind his Analytical Engine, a machine that could be programmed with a set of instructions, that could process the mathematics involved, and that could output the result on paper, remains at the core of modern computing.

SPEED AND POWER

Since the days of the 30-ton ENIAC computers have been shrinking in size and increasing power in and speed—all because of the electronic revolution started in 1948 by the team headed by American scientist Walter H. Brattain (1902–88).

Before then, electronic devices (such as the radio) depended on delicate glass-and-metal valves to control and amplify the flow of electricity in their circuits. Brattain's brainchild was the transistor, a device that, because it was smaller, tougher, and used less power, started to replace the valve. Once production got underway, transistors became far cheaper, too. Among the first wave of popular transistorized devices were the pocket-sized radios of the early 1960s—people could now listen to their favorite music station or the latest news from a radio no bigger than the palm of their hands.

The next step toward today's computers was the integrated circuit. Even though transistors were small, they were still wired together in the old-fashioned way.

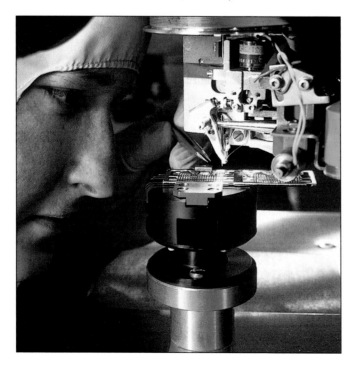

▶ Making an IC chip requires surgically clean conditions. The slightest particle falling onto a microcircuit renders it useless.

The integrated circuit, or IC, puts transistors, together with other components and their connections, on a single wafer of silicon material, the silicon chip. American electronics engineer Jack Kilby made the first integrated circuit in 1958, though an attempt at onc using valve technology had been made by a German firm back in 1926. However, Kilby's components still had to be joined by hand. In 1959, a team headed by Robert Noyce discovered how to make an IC chip using the newly developed planar process. This uses photographic techniques to create the tiny circuit patterns that go on each chip.

Noyce's team managed to put just one transistor on its first silicon chip; a typical IC chip of today packs thousands of components on a piece of material just a few millimeters square. Compared with a valve, only a tiny amount of heat is generated; even so, a desktop computer generally needs a fan to keep the circuits cool. Microchip technology has led to a host of cheap and reliable communications devices including portable telephones, miniature televisions, CD players, and many others.

◀ A microscope-view of a silicon chip, the heart of a computer. Nearly half a million components are squeezed onto a space half the size of a thumbnail.

CD-ROM AND MULTIMEDIA

High-power and low-cost computing has led to another communications revolution, multimedia, in which words, sounds, pictures, and movies are combined in one electronic document. Using a multimedia encyclopedia, you can read about something, hear the noise it makes, and see a short section of video. This makes multimedia a powerful learning tool, a giant leap from the printed word. Not that publications such as books and magazines are likely to disappear—multimedia is an additional communications tool, rather than a direct replacement.

▶ Inside a CD player. The laser beam (shown in red) reads the spiral of pits buried in the underside of the compact disc.

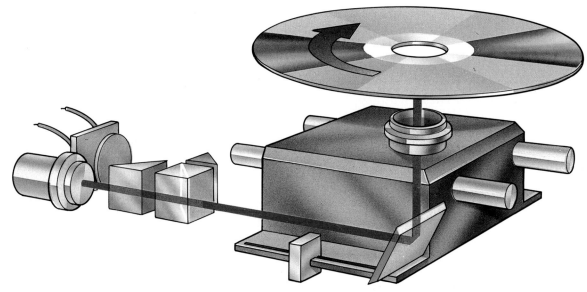

As computers get more powerful, the programs for them get more complex, and the demand for storage capacity gets bigger, too. Until the early 1990s, floppy disks containing information in magnetic form were enough for most purposes. But programs now need a new storage medium, the CD-ROM, which stands for **c**ompact **d**isc, **r**ead-**o**nly **m**emory, meaning that a computer can read the information on the disc but cannot record onto it. A program is stored as a coded spiral of tiny pits, buried in the plastic material of the disc. On a typical 120 mm-wide disc there are millions of pits—if you unwound the spiral, it would stretch about 3 miles! A low-power laser beam reads the digital code into the computer. Each CD-ROM can store hundreds of times as much information as a conventional floppy disk.

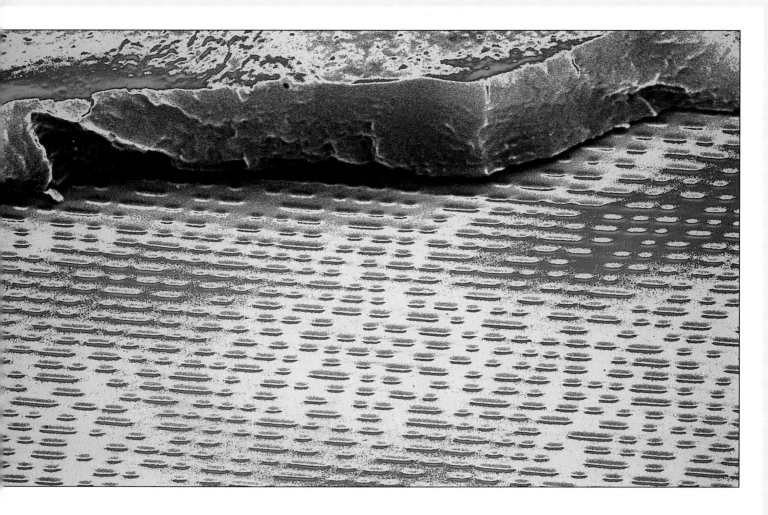

The CD-ROM is based on the audio compact disc, invented by engineers at the Dutch Philips company in the late 1970s. In 1980, Philips joined up with Sony of Japan, and the two companies brought out the first CDs soon after, aimed at the well-heeled hi-fi enthusiast. The CD has now almost entirely replaced the pressed-vinyl disk used on the old record players.

CD-ROMs may be the best way of presenting information on screen, but if you want to search for information yourself, then one of the best tools could be the Internet. This is a network of tens of thousands of computers, spanning the globe. It is used by individuals, universities, commercial organizations, and government departments. People using the Internet number 25 million or more, a figure that is rising all the time.

On the Internet you can find details of any subject you care to name. In fact, the ocean of information is so vast that the biggest difficulty can be finding things – you often need a special tracker program to hunt down a particular information source. As well as using the Internet as a vast library, people also talk to each other on it, a sort of electronic pen-pal system. Various codes and signals are used by Internet users, including "smileys" such as this one – :-). Look at this page sideways to see if the author is happy!

☀ NEW FRONTIERS

Computers have already linked the world together in a global information network, and it is likely that more people and computers will become joined in the future. This electronic sea of information is called cyberspace, a term coined by Canadian science-fiction writer William Gibson in the 1980s. Gibson foresees a future in which we will be able to submerge in this "parallel universe," using computer-imaging machinery to make it look and feel as real as the everyday world around us.

Virtual reality—VR—is a technology that provides the essential link with the electronic world of cyberspace. Wearing a pair of VR goggles for vision and a VR glove for touch, you can enter a computer program as if it were real life. The most popular use for VR so far is for gaming, where you can, for example, "fly" a fast jet without ever leaving the ground.

▲ LunaCorps moon vehicle, designed for do-it-yourself drivers on the moon.

One commercial company is following up the VR idea with an interactive space exploration plan. LunaCorps aims to launch a moon vehicle by Russian rocket in 1997, landing it at the site where Neil Armstrong first stepped on the moon in 1969. Some science experiments are planned for the vehicle, but for most of the time, people will pay to drive it around the moon using video links and VR goggles.

Computers that recognize speech and handwriting are already in use, though they need to be improved dramatically before the finger-operated keyboard becomes extinct. And now there is a worldwide race to produce thought-controlled computers. The American Brainlink system is one of the first results of this race. The brain's tiny electrical impulses are picked up by sensors attached to the head and are then relayed to the Brainlink computer.

Among the things that Brainlink can do is to help athletes improve their performances. Apparently, people can be trained to produce types of brain patterns that improve their chances of winning. It is a short step from this to being able to use Brainlink for steering a vehicle, and the advantages for disabled people could be enormous. At present the machine uses wire connectors, but soon long-range radio equipment may allow thought-control at a distance.

▲ VR goggles help this biochemist visualize a complex molecular structure.

 **HANDHELD HELPERS**

Personal digital assistants, or PDAs, will become popular in the future. As yet, the handheld PDAs are limited in what they can do (the Apple Newton is one of the first), but future models will recognize handwriting and speech and will communicate with other computers anywhere via satellite links.

CHRONOLOGY OF ADVANCE

Here are some of the people, discoveries, inventions, and improvements that have brought about the world of today.

Ancient Egypt (about 3000 B.C.) Hieroglyphic picture writing and papyrus writing material developed. The first hieroglyphics date back to about 3000 B.C.; the latest example was from about A.D. 394. An even earlier form of picture writing was the cuneiform script used by the Sumerians about 4000 B.C.

Ancient China (about A.D. 105) First use of papermaking. Early forms of printing developed.

Johannes Gutenberg German printer (about 1400-68). Invented the European printing press with movable type after experiments in the 1440s. His most famous work was the Mazarin Bible, which he produced with Johann Fust.

William Caxton English printer (about 1422-91). Learned about printing from Gutenberg and set up the first printing press in England in 1476. Printed about 100 different titles, including works by Geoffrey Chaucer and translations of the Roman statesman Cicero.

Blaise Pascal French mathematician and physicist (1623-62). Made the world's first mechanical calculator in 1642. Also studied the effects of pressure and invented the hydraulic press.

Robert Hooke British scientist (1635-1703). Investigated, among other things, the elasticity of materials (such as springs) and invented the universal joint. Suggested a type of telephone involving two cans joined by a length of string or wire.

Claude Chappe French engineer (1763-1805). Devised an optical telegraph for the French military. It was the first system to be called a telegraph, from the Greek words *tele*, meaning "far," and *graphein*, "to write." Other telegraph pioneers include Paul Schilling, who devised an electric telegraph and built a line in Russia in the 1830s.

Jean-François Champollion French scholar (1790-1832).

Cracked the secrets of the three forms of early writing inscribed in the ancient Egyptian Rosetta Stone. His approach to translation work was criticized for many years, and it was not until the 1860s that other archaeologists admitted that his techniques worked.

Samuel Morse American inventor (1791-1872). Devised the dot-dash code system for the electric telegraph, first demonstrating it in 1837. It has since become the international standard.

Charles Babbage Mathematics professor (1792-1871). A pioneer of computing who designed a pair of machines intended to speed up mathematical calculations. Highly regarded as a computing pioneer.

Joseph Henry American teacher and physicist (1797-1878). A pioneer of electricity research, he invented a type of electric telegraph and the first practical electric motor. He became the first director of the Smithsonian Institution, in Washington, DC.

Charles Wheatstone British scientist (1802-75). Invented a practical electric telegraph with William Cooke in 1837. He also devised a viewer for three-dimensional pictures.

Louis Braille French teacher (1809-52). Devised the raised-dot system by which blind people can read books in 1829. Braille himself was blind. The earliest raised-letter printing was thought up by Valentin Haüy (1745-1822).

Julius Reuter German news gatherer (1816-99). First worked as a bank clerk. In 1849, began sending stock exchange prices in Europe, first by carrier pigeon, then by electric telegraph. Opened a news agency office in London in 1851.

Alexander Graham Bell Scottish-American teacher and inventor (1847-1922). Invented the first telephone in 1876, which worked by changing sound into electrical signals and back again into sound. Thomas Edison soon produced a better design, which was much more successful.

Thomas Alva Edison American inventor (1847-1931). A prolific inventor who took out 1,097 patents. Invented the first phonograph in 1877, using money from another invention of his, a telegraphic printer.

Heinrich Rudolf Hertz German physicist (1857-94). First person to broadcast and receive radio waves, in 1887, using specially developed electric-spark equipment.

Guglielmo Marconi Italian scientist (1874-1937). Invented the wireless telegraph, a system that could send messages over long distances without wires. In 1901 his radio equipment transmitted Morse code signals across the Atlantic Ocean, from Cornwall, England, to Newfoundland, Canada.

John Logie Baird Scottish engineer (1888-1946). In 1924 he became the first person to transmit a television picture using radio waves, and in 1928 he was the first to send a picture across the Atlantic. Despite these early successes, Baird's mechanical TV scanner was beaten commercially by the system developed by Vladimir Zworykin.

Vladimir Zworykin Russian-American physicist and electronics engineer (1889-1982). Helped develop the television camera and picture tube. The electronic TV system was a big improvement over Baird's scanner. Zworykin also developed the electron microscope, a vastly more powerful machine than the traditional type.

Robert Alexander Watson-Watt British engineer (1892-1973). Developed radar, filing a patent for radio direction-finding in 1919. In 1935 he headed a team to "develop a system for locating aircraft in all weathers and by day or night by radio waves," what was later to be generally known as radar. His work was of great value in World War II. After the war, Watson-Watt developed radar for peaceful uses.

Chester Carlson American patent lawyer (1906-68). Devised the xerographic system of dry-copying. His first copy was made in 1938, but the first commercial copiers using his system were not produced until the 1950s. It is now the most widely used copy system of all.

William Bradford Shockley English-American physicist (1910-89). Together with fellow scientists John Bardeen and Walter H. Brattain, invented the transistor in 1947, opening the way for the electronic world of today.

Arthur C. Clarke Science fact and fiction writer (1917-). First thought up the idea of using satellites for long-distance communications, in 1945. Since then, has written many books on futuristic themes and has had movies made of several of his books, including the classic *2001: A Space Odyssey*, filmed by director Stanley Kubrick. Other influential writers include the Canadian William Gibson, whose "cyberpunk" style previews the computerized world of the near future.

◀ **Vladimir Zworykin**

43

GLOSSARY

Archaeology Scientific study of the life of ancient peoples, carried out principally by excavating the sites of cities and dwellings.

Binary code Counting system used by computers, consisting of "strings" of codes that use combinations of just two numbers or digits, 0 and 1. Any device (such as a computer) that uses this system is known as a digital machine.

Braille System of raised letter code, to make reading possible for blind people. It was invented by Louis Braille in the nineteenth century.

Carbon microphone Type of microphone commonly used in telephones.

Cathode-ray tube The familiar TV display system as used in the home and for computer and radar screens. Streams of electrons from the rear of the tube hit the inside of the front, where a special coating causes the screen to glow. Often abbreviated as CRT. The latest picture tube system uses thousands of miniaturized CRTs to provide the picture, instead of just one. The result? A tube just 4 inches thick.

CCD Charge coupled device, as used in camcorders. The CCD uses an array of up to 800,000 tiny light sensors, all mounted on an individual imaging chip, usually about 17 mm (7 inches) across. The sensors convert the light falling on them to an electric current, larger or smaller, depending on the intensity of light. This is fed into the camcorder's complex circuits, eventually to be recorded on video tape.

CD-ROM Compact disc-read only memory. The latest type of compact disc, especially suited to store computer information for multimedia presentations. It stores the digital information as a spiral of microscopically small pits in the disc.

Comsat Communications satellite designed as a relay station in space for radio and TV signals. The first artificial satellite, the Russian *Sputnik I*, was launched in 1957; there are now hundreds of satellites in orbit, their functions ranging from communications duties to "sky spy" photographic missions for military purposes.

Cyberspace Term for the "ocean" of computerized information that is

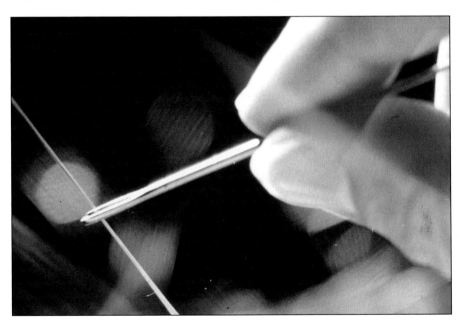

▲ The increasing amount of information being passed around the world is overloading conventional telephone lines. To cope with demand, "information superhighways" of a material called fiber optics are being laid. These fibers can carry over 30,000 times more information than a telephone wire of the same width.

now available for users. The word comes from cybernetics (from the Greek *kybernetes*, meaning "helmsman"), which compares complex computer systems with the human nervous system.

Earth station The ground link between the user and a Comsat. Earth stations can be spotted by their satellite dishes.

Electric telegraph Long-distance communications system that uses electricity passing down a wire. Various types were developed, mostly in the nineteenth century.

Electromagnet A magnet consisting of a soft iron core around which a coil of insulated wire is wound. If a current is passed down the wire, the core is magnetized.

Electronics The study of devices that depend on the controlled flow of electrons (tiny parts of atoms) to make them work.

Electrostatics The study of electric charges that are at rest and the forces that act among them. Examples of electrostatic attraction include that between a rubber balloon and small pieces of fluff and paper.

Geostationary orbit An orbit used by many Comsats, some 22,000 miles above Earth's equator, where the speed of a satellite matches the speed of Earth's rotation. The result is that the satellite remains in one spot above Earth.

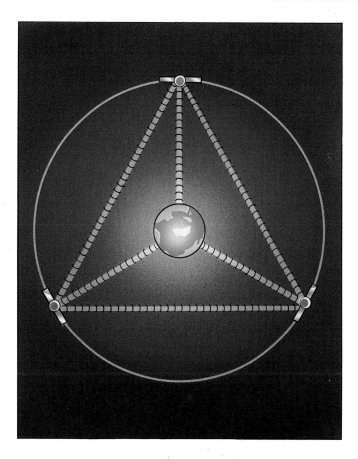

◀ Situated 36,000 miles above the equator, a trio of comsats in geostationary orbit covers all the globe except the poles.

Hieroglyphics A method of writing that used pictures and symbols to represent words and sounds. Used especially in ancient Egypt.

Iconoscope The electronic picture tube invented by Vladimir Zworykin. It competed with John Logie Baird's mechanical scanner system in the early days of television.

Integrated circuit A miniature electronic circuit, widely used in electronic equipment such as computers and calculators. Integrated circuits are often referred to simply as IC "chips."

Internet Global network of linked computers. Used as a library, bulletin board, and general communications tool by computer users.

Laser Beam of intense light. Unlike ordinary light, laser light is "coherent"—the light is one pure color and the rays move in parallel lines. This means that a laser beam remains as a tight beam and does not spread out like, for example, a flashlight. Lasers do not have to be powerful to be useful, however—a compact disc player uses a very low-power laser to read information on the disc.

Modem A machine that converts computer data into a form that can be transmitted down a telephone line. It can also be used to receive information.

Mongols of Asia A powerful empire, based in the heart of eastern Asia, that grew to great power in the thirteenth century under the command of Genghis Khan. The Mongols used a horse relay system to carry urgent communications, an idea copied by the Pony Express between 1860 and 1861.

Morse code Dot-dash alphabet first devised by Samuel Morse in 1837. It was very useful for the electric telegraph, but is also used to communicate by radio, flag, and lamp.

Multimedia Electronic document, usually delivered on CD-ROM, that presents information in words, pictures, movies, and sounds.

Nobel Prize Five annual awards, given for the best work in physics, chemistry, medicine, literature, and the cause of universal peace. Alfred Nobel, a Swedish inventor and chemist who had made a fortune from explosives and oil, left a major portion of his estate to be given as awards. He died in 1896 and the prizes were first awarded in 1901.

Papyrus African plant that grows to a height of three to ten feet. The ancient Egyptians, Greeks, and Romans used the fibers of this plant to make writing material.

Patent A right to make and sell an invention without competition from others who might try to copy it. Patent applications are made through patent offices, where they are carefully checked to make sure that they are for new and original ideas. Patents must be obtained in every country where protection is required.

PDA Personal digital assistant, the name for hand-held computer organizers. Typically, a PDA has a small screen, can plug into a modem and bigger computers and has some form of handwriting recognition ability – necessary because it has no keyboard.

Printed circuit board Piece of material on which all or most of an electronic device's circuits are wired together. Particularly useful, as PCBs can often be slotted in and out of a machine, making repairs quick and easy.

Radio wave One part of the electromagnetic spectrum, which includes radio, visible light, and X rays. Such electromagnetic waves travel at the speed of light, 186,262 miles per second.

Solar cell An electric device that produces electricity from the energy in sunlight.

Telegraph Device for sending messages long distances. It uses an electric current that passes along a wire linking a transmitter and receiver.

◀ **One of the first PDAs, the Apple Newton of 1993.**

Television format Type of transmission system. There are three main TV formats in the world. NTSC is used in North America and Japan. PAL offers a crisper picture and is used in much of the rest of the world. SECAM is used in France and some east European countries.

Teleworker Person who uses electronic telecommunications equipment to avoid the need to travel to an office every day.

Telex A communication device which uses typewriters linked by telephone lines; what is typed on one can be sent to another.

Transistor Tiny device that can act as a switch or amplifier in an electric circuit. Transistors are basic components in electronic equipment.

Vacuum tube Electronic component, such as a valve or cathode-ray tube, that has had the air extracted from its interior.

Valve Device for controlling the flow of electricity in an electrical circuit. Valves have now been almost universally replaced by transistors, which are smaller, cheaper, and more reliable.

Video format The size, shape, and electronic type of a particular recording system. The VHS format from the J. Victor Company of Japan is the type that is most widely used in home video cassette recorders. TV companies use others, all of higher quality. For domestic camcorders, VHS and 8 mm are used, both also made in high-band versions that offer improved picture quality.

▲ **In Great Britain, television programs were first broadcast in 1937, from London's Alexandra Palace transmitter, shown here.**

☀ FURTHER READING

Balcziak, B. *Radio.* Communication: Today and Tomorrow. Vero Beach, FL: Rourke Corp., 1989.

Hill, John. *Exploring Information Technology.* Exploring Science. Milwaukee: Raintree Steck-Vaughn, 1992.

Lampton, Christopher. *Telecommunications: From Telegraph to Modems.* Venture Books. New York: Franklin Watts, 1991.

Lampton, Christopher. *Thomas Alva Edison.* North Bellmore, NY: Marshall Cavendish Corp., 1991.

Morgan, Nina. *Guglielmo Marconi.* Pioneers of Science. New York: Bookwright Press, 1991.

Quiri, Patricia Ryon. *Alexander Graham Bell.* First Books. New York: Franklin Watts, 1991.

Sauvain, Philip. *Communications.* Breakthrough. Milwaukee: Raintree Steck-Vaughn, 1993.

Time/Life Books. *The Computer Age.* Understanding Science & Nature. Mahwah, NJ: Silver Burdett, 1992.

Weeks, Jessica V. *Television.* New York: Crestwood House, 1994.

MAGAZINES

Popular Mechanics
Box 7170
Red Oak, IA 51591

Popular Science
Box 5100
Harlan, IA 51563

Scientific American
415 Madison Avenue
New York, NY 10017

INDEX

DATE DUE